# Symbols of the United States

### by Etta Johnson

## Table of Contents

# ☆Introduction☆

A **symbol** makes us think of something. This statue is a symbol. What does this statue make us think of?

The United States has many symbols. What do the symbols make us think of?

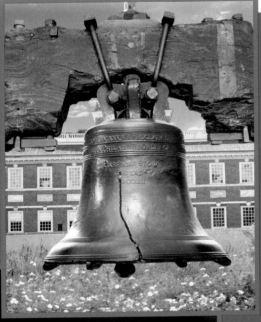

## Words to Know

bald eagle

Declaration of Independence

freedom

Liberty Bell

Statue of Liberty

symbol

See the Glossary on page 22.

# What Is the Flag of the United States?

The flag is a symbol of the United States. We look at the flag. We think about the United States.

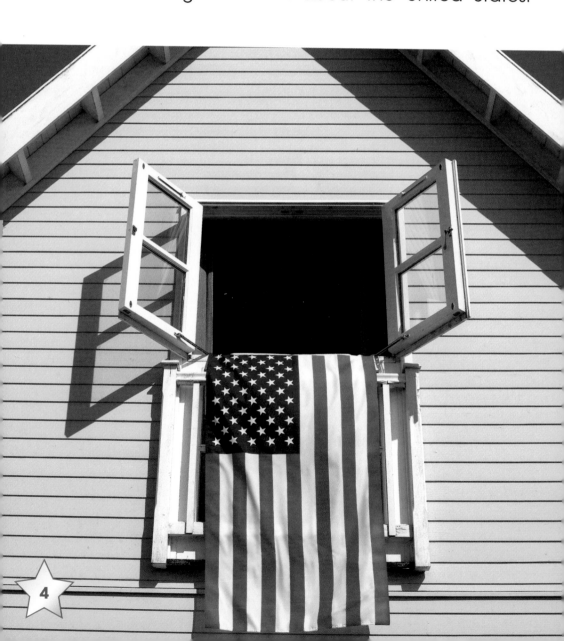

The first U.S. flag had 13 stars and 13 stripes. They were symbols of the first 13 states.

Now the flag has 50 stars. The stars are symbols of the 50 states.

13 stars and 13 stripes

50 stars and 13 stripes

People to Know

Some people say that Betsy Ross made the first U.S. flag.

You can see the flag in many places. Where else do you see the flag?

We show respect for our flag. How can you show respect?

People in the United States say the Pledge of Allegiance to the flag. These words show respect.

# What Is the Statue of Liberty?

The **Statue of Liberty** is a symbol of the United States. It makes us think of **freedom.**

▲ **The Statue of Liberty is in New York Harbor.**

Many people came to the United States. Many people came on ships. They saw the Statue of Liberty. The Statue of Liberty welcomed them.

People to Know

Emma Lazarus wrote a famous poem that is on the base of the statue. Her words welcome people to the United States.

Now people come from around the world. They want to visit the Statue of Liberty.

MISS FREEDOM
NEW YORK

The Statue of Liberty is very big. The nose is 4.5 feet (1.37 meters) long.

torch

crown

height:
151 feet
(46 meters)

base

## Learn More...

Visit Liberty Island
in New York.
Look for pictures of
the Statue of Liberty.
Visit the Web site
www.nps.gov/stli.

# What Is the Liberty Bell?

The **Liberty Bell** is a symbol of the United States. It makes us think of freedom.

The Liberty Bell rang in 1776. People came running.

A man read the **Declaration of Independence** to them. The United States was free!

You can see the Liberty Bell in Philadelphia. It is cracked. The bell cannot ring now.

▲ The Liberty Bell Center is in Philadelphia.

The Liberty Bell is very big. It weighs 2,080 pounds (943 kilograms).

crack

height
3 feet
(.2 meters)

Crack length:
24.5 inches
(62.2 centimeters)

clapper

▲ The Liberty Bell weighs 2,080 pounds.

# What Is the Bald Eagle?

The **bald eagle** is a symbol of the United States. It makes us think of freedom. The bald eagle is on the Great Seal of the United States.

▼ the Great Seal of the United States

The president signs important papers. The papers have the Great Seal.

Where else do you see the bald eagle?

IT'S A
FACT

The bald eagle is
in danger. Today
no one can harm
an eagle.

Bald eagles fly fast. They have 7,000 feathers to help them! A bald eagle can fly 30 miles (48 kilometers) per hour.

Bald eagles weigh 8 to 12 pounds (3.5 to 5.4 kilograms).

7 feet (2 meters)

 How many miles (kilometers) can a bald eagle fly in 30 minutes?

ANSWER: 15 MILES (24 KILOMETERS)

Tell about three symbols of the United States.

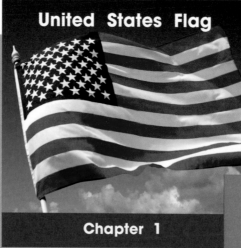

United States Flag

Chapter 1

## Symbols of the United State

Liberty Bell

Chapter 3

## THINK ABOUT IT

1. Which symbols do you see at your school? What do they mean?

**Statue of Liberty**

**Chapter 2**

**Bald Eagle**

**Chapter 4**

2. Which United States symbol is most important to you?

**bald eagle** a big, strong bird with a white head

*The **bald eagle** flies in the sky.*

**Declaration of Independence** the paper that says the United States is free

*You can see the **Declaration of Independence** in Washington, D.C.*

**freedom** the liberty to do and say what you want

*People in the United States have the **freedom** to say what they think.*

**Liberty Bell** a bell that is a symbol of freedom in the United States

*The **Liberty Bell** rang in 1776.*

**Statue of Liberty** the statue that welcomes people to the United States

*The **Statue of Liberty** is in New York Harbor.*

**symbol** an object or picture that represents something

*The flag is a special **symbol** of the United States.*